LISA LESLIE

BASKETBALL LEGEND

BY LUKE HANLON

Book design by Jake Nordby
Cover design by Jake Nordby

Photographs ©: Matt York/AP Images, cover, 1; Lisa Blumenfeld/WNBAE/Getty Images Sport/ Getty Images, 4, 7; Tony Duffy/Allsport/Hulton Archive/Getty Images, 8, 14; Ken Levine/ Allsport/Getty Images Sport/Getty Images, 11; Gary Newkirk/Allsport/Hulton Archive/Getty Images, 12; Rick Stewart/Allsport/Getty Images Sport/Getty Images, 17; Harry How/Allsport/ Getty Images Sport/Getty Images, 19; Michael Caulfield/AP Images, 20–21; Mark J. Terrill/ AP Images, 22, 30; Lucy Nicholson/AP Images, 24; Streeter Lecka/Getty Images Sport/Getty Images, 27; Red Line Editorial, 29

Press Box Books, an imprint of Press Room Editions.

ISBN
978-1-63494-790-9 (library bound)
978-1-63494-810-4 (paperback)
978-1-63494-849-4 (epub)
978-1-63494-830-2 (hosted ebook)

Library of Congress Control Number: 2023909014

Distributed by North Star Editions, Inc.
2297 Waters Drive
Mendota Heights, MN 55120
www.northstareditions.com

Printed in the United States of America
012024

About the Author
Luke Hanlon is a sportswriter and editor based in Minneapolis.

TABLE OF CONTENTS

1 HIGH RISER

Early in Lisa Leslie's career, she wrote down a list of goals. One of those goals was to dunk in a game. She tried to do it in 1997, during the first Women's National Basketball Association (WNBA) game, but she missed. Five years later, another opportunity presented itself.

Leslie's Los Angeles Sparks battled the Miami Sol on July 30, 2002. In the first half, Leslie defended a Sol player shooting a three-pointer. The shot didn't go in, and Sparks forward Latasha Byears grabbed

Lisa Leslie averaged 16.9 points per game during the 2002 season.

the rebound. Already near half-court, Leslie was all alone.

Byears saw her teammate and quickly tossed an outlet pass to Leslie. She caught the ball with no Sol players around her. This was the moment she had been waiting for. After taking two dribbles, Leslie leaped off her left foot with the ball in her right hand. She slammed the ball through the rim for the first dunk in WNBA history.

The crowd went wild. Fans in the Staples Center rose to their feet in excitement. Leslie raised both arms in the air and ran to half-court. Her teammate Tamecka Dixon jumped into her arms in celebration. After years of brilliance on the court, one of the WNBA's biggest stars had delivered again.

Leslie runs to celebrate with her teammates after dunking against the Sol.

2 CALIFORNIA KID

Lisa Leslie was born on July 7, 1972, in Gardena, California. She grew up in nearby Compton, California, which is south of Los Angeles. Her father, Walter, was a basketball player. However, he left Lisa's mother, Christine, while she was pregnant with Lisa.

To make enough money for her kids, Christine worked as a truck driver. That meant that she was away from home for weeks at a time. While Christine was gone, Lisa lived with other family members.

Lisa Leslie played for Morningside High School from 1986 to 1990.

Christine was 6-foot-3 (191 cm), and she passed her height down to Lisa. While Lisa was growing up, kids picked on her for being the tallest girl in school. People would constantly ask her if she played basketball because of her height. The answer was no until middle school. As a 12-year-old, Lisa was 6 feet (183 cm) tall. One of her classmates asked her to play for the middle school team. Hoping to make new friends, Lisa agreed to play.

It didn't take long to see that Lisa was a gifted basketball player. By the time she was in eighth grade, she played on the boys' team. Lisa went on to play on the girls' team at Morningside High School. As a sophomore, she helped her team get to the state championship game. Playing against Oakland Fremont, Lisa missed a game-winning shot, and her team lost.

Leslie played college basketball from 1990 to 1994.

While the miss haunted Lisa, it motivated her to get better. The next year, Morningside played Oakland Fremont again, and Lisa scored 21 points to secure the state championship.

USC had a record of 89-31 when Leslie played there.

Lisa almost made history during her senior year. On February 7, 1990, she scored 101 points in just 16 minutes of a game. The national high school record was 105 points. Lisa would have shattered the record, but the opposing team's coach forfeited the game at halftime.

Coaches from more than 100 colleges reached out to Lisa about joining their schools. She decided to stay close to home and play basketball at the University of Southern California (USC). Leslie was a force in college right away, as she was named the National Freshman of the Year in 1991. After her senior season in 1994, she won the Naismith College Player of the Year award. Her basketball legacy in California would only grow from there.

FOCUS ON EDUCATION

Lisa Leslie played at USC for four years and graduated with a bachelor's degree in communications. While she played professional basketball for years after college, she wasn't done with her education. Leslie finished her master's degree in business administration at the University of Phoenix while she was in the WNBA.

3 STAYING HOME

When Lisa Leslie was done with college, there was no professional basketball league for women in the United States. While she couldn't play professionally in her country, she could play for the United States on the international stage. In 1994, Leslie played for the US team for the first time at that year's World Championship. The Americans hadn't lost a game in that tournament in 11 years. However, they lost to Brazil in the semifinals and settled

Leslie played in three World Championships for the United States.

for bronze. With the 1996 Olympics coming up in Atlanta, USA Basketball knew it needed to win gold.

Before the Olympics, the US team went on a 52-game tour around the world. With a roster built around Leslie, the Americans won all 52 games. Then, in the Olympics, Leslie led the team in scoring. The team went undefeated in Atlanta and won Olympic gold.

The popularity of the US team led to the creation of the WNBA, which began play in 1997. Leslie joined her hometown team, the Los Angeles Sparks. As she'd done in high school and college, Leslie found

SCORING MACHINE

Lisa Leslie was dominant at the 1996 Olympics. In a win against Japan in the quarterfinals, Leslie scored 35 points. No US player had ever scored that many points in an Olympic game. Leslie scored a total of 156 points in the Olympics that year, setting a new record for an American player.

Leslie (third from left) sings "The Star-Spangled Banner" after winning gold at the 1996 Olympics.

success right away. Standing 6-foot-5 (196 cm), she used her height to dominate in the post on offense and defense. While Leslie was left-handed, she could also use her right hand just as effectively. She had skills like a guard even though she played center.

In 1999, Leslie's play helped the Sparks make the playoffs for the first time. But the Houston Comets swept the Sparks in the conference finals. The same result happened the next season, as the Comets went on to win their fourth championship in a row.

Leslie came back on a mission in 2001. She led the Sparks to a 28-4 record in the regular season and won the WNBA Most Valuable Player (MVP) Award. In the playoffs, the Sparks faced Houston in the first round. This time, the Sparks swept the Comets. Los Angeles made it to the WNBA Finals and played the Charlotte Sting. Leslie scored 24 points in both games of the series to help the Sparks win their first championship.

Leslie looks to score in the 2001 WNBA Finals.

WE GOT NEXT

Set to launch in 1997, the WNBA needed stars to promote the league. There were plenty of options to choose from after the 1996 Olympics. The league decided on three players from the US team that won gold: Sheryl Swoopes of the Houston Comets, Rebecca Lobo of the New York Liberty, and Lisa Leslie.

To build excitement for the new league, the WNBA ran a commercial in 1996 featuring the three stars. It showed them walking into an arena with WNBA duffel bags. The commercial ended with the league's slogan, "We Got Next," on the screen, as well as the date for the league's first game.

That first game was held on June 21, 1997. It featured Leslie's Sparks and Lobo's Liberty. Both players scored 16 points, and the Liberty won 67–57. Leslie's skill and charisma led to her being one of the league's biggest stars throughout her career.

Leslie (9) and Kym Hampton (34) take part in the first jump ball in WNBA history.

4 LA LEGEND

Lisa Leslie's talent had helped turn the Sparks into the best team in the WNBA. Los Angeles finished the 2002 season with the best record in the league yet again. That year, Leslie also became the first player to dunk in a WNBA game. She inspired future generations of players to dream of playing above the rim.

The Sparks were just as dominant in the 2002 playoffs. So was Leslie, as she averaged 19.3 points and 7.8 rebounds per game while making 54 percent of

Leslie averaged at least 15 points per game in all 12 WNBA seasons that she played.

Leslie hoists the WNBA championship trophy and the WNBA Finals MVP Award in 2002.

her shot attempts. The Sparks went 6-0 in the postseason and repeated as WNBA champions. Just as in 2001, Leslie won the Finals MVP Award.

For the rest of her WNBA career, Leslie remained one of the league's brightest stars. She went on to win the MVP Award again in 2004. Then in 2006, she averaged a career-high 20 points per game. She also made more than 50 percent of her regular-season shot attempts for the first time in her career. Those stats earned her another MVP Award.

While her WNBA career was winding down, Leslie competed in her fourth and final Olympics in Beijing, China, in 2008. At 36 years old, she started in all eight games. Her play helped the United States win gold again. Leslie became just

DUNKING MENTOR

After Lisa Leslie dunked, no WNBA player did so in a game until 2008. That year, the Los Angeles Sparks selected Candace Parker with the top pick in the WNBA Draft. In June, Parker dunked on the same basket that Leslie had first dunked on six years prior. She did it as Leslie's teammate.

the second American to ever win four Olympic gold medals in basketball. She finished her international career with a record of 220-14 and a perfect 32-0 mark in the Olympics.

Leslie retired from the WNBA in 2009 as the league's all-time leading scorer and rebounder. After her playing career, she made more history in 2011 when she became a partial owner of the Los Angeles Sparks. Leslie was the first former player to invest in a WNBA team. In 2015, she was inducted into the Basketball Hall of Fame for the amazing legacy she left on the game. Many stars have passed through the WNBA. Only a handful have had as much of an impact on the league as Leslie.

Leslie blocked 11 shots in eight games at the 2008 Olympics.

TIMELINE

1. **Gardena, California (July 7, 1972)**
   Lisa Leslie is born.

2. **Torrance, California (February 7, 1990)**
   Leslie scores 101 points in the first half of a high school game.

3. **Los Angeles, California (April 1994)**
   Leslie wins the Naismith College Player of the Year award after her senior year at USC.

4. **Atlanta, Georgia (August 4, 1996)**
   Leslie helps the United States win an Olympic gold medal after beating Brazil.

5. **Inglewood, California (June 21, 1997)**
   Leslie plays in the first game in WNBA history.

6. **Manhattan, New York (July 14, 1999)**
   Leslie plays in the first All-Star Game in WNBA history and is voted the game's MVP.

7. **Los Angeles, California (September 1, 2001)**
   Leslie lifts the Sparks to their first WNBA championship.

8. **Beijing, China (August 23, 2008)**
   Leslie becomes the second American to win four Olympic gold medals in basketball after she helps the United States beat Australia.

MAP

Birth date: July 7, 1972

Birthplace:
Gardena, California

Position: Center

Size: 6-foot-5 (196 cm),
170 pounds (77 kg)

Teams: USC Trojans
(1990–94), USA Basketball
Women's National Team
(1993–2008), Los Angeles
Sparks (1997–2009)

Major awards: WNBA Finals
MVP (2001, 2002), WNBA
MVP (2001, 2004, 2006),
WNBA Defensive Player of the Year (2004, 2008), Olympic gold
medalist (1996, 2000, 2004, 2008)

GLOSSARY

conference
A smaller group of teams that make up part of a sports league.

draft
An event that allows teams to choose new players coming into the league.

legacy
The way a person is remembered, as well as the changes they helped to make.

outlet pass
A pass made by a player after a rebound to start a fast break.

post
The area close to the basket where taller players usually play.

postseason
Another word for playoffs; the time after the end of the regular season when teams play to determine a champion.

swept
Won every game in a series.

World Championship
An international tournament held every four years.

TO LEARN MORE

Books

Fishman, Jon. *Tina Charles vs. Lisa Leslie: Who Would Win?* Minneapolis: Lerner Publications, 2024.

Lowe, Alexander. *G.O.A.T. Basketball Centers*. Minneapolis: Lerner Publications, 2023.

O'Neal, Ciara. *The WNBA Finals*. Mendota Heights, MN: Apex Editions, 2023.

More Information

To learn more about Lisa Leslie, go to **pressboxbooks.com/AllAccess**.

These links are routinely monitored and updated to provide the most current information available.

INDEX